Date: 4/4/12

Electric Animals

by Natalie Lunis

Consultant: Mark Nelson, Ph.D.
Professor of Molecular and Integrative Physiology
Beckman Institute
Neuroscience Program
University of Illinois, Urbana-Champaign

BEARPORT
PUBLISHING

New York, New York

Credits

Cover and Title Page, © Angel M. Fitor/OSF/Photolibrary, © Max Gibbs/OSF/Photolibrary, © Patrice Ceisel/Visuals Unlimited, Inc., © Jane Burton/Nature Picture Library, and © Gerald Nowak/WaterFrame/Photolibrary; 4TL, © Marilyn & Maris Kazmers/SeaPics; 4TR, © Pat Morris/Ardea; 4B, © Norbert Wu/Minden Pictures/Getty Images; 5T, © Pacific Stock/SuperStock; 5B, © Dave Watts/Nature Picture Library; 6, © D. R. Schrichte/SeaPics; 7, © Johnny Jensen/Image Quest Marine; 8, © Doug Perrine/SeaPics; 9, © David B. Fleetham/OSF/Photolibrary; 10, © Norbert Wu/Minden Pictures; 11, © Angel M. Fitor/OSF/Photolibrary; 12, © David B. Snyder/SeaPics; 13, © Norbert Wu/Science Faction; 15T, © Dante Fenolio/Photo Researchers, Inc.; 15B, © Zigmund Leszczynski/Animals Animals Earth Scenes; 16, © Jane Burton/Nature Picture Library; 17, © Jean Michel Labat/Ardea; 18, © Mike Parry/Minden Pictures; 19, © Pacific Stock/SuperStock; 20L, © Ken Lucas/Ardea; 20R, © Reg Morrison/Auscape/Minden Pictures; 21, © Dave Watts/Alamy; 22T, © Doug Perrine/SeaPics; 22M, © Dante Fenolio/Photo Researchers, Inc.; 22B, © Georgette Douwma/Nature Picture Library; 23, © Jeroen Visser/Shutterstock.

Publisher: Kenn Goin
Editorial Director: Adam Siegel
Creative Director: Spencer Brinker
Design: Dawn Beard Creative
Photo Researcher: Picture Perfect Professionals, LLC

Library of Congress Cataloging-in-Publication Data

Lunis, Natalie.
  Electric animals / by Natalie Lunis.
     p. cm. — (Animals with super powers)
  Includes bibliographical references and index.
  ISBN-13: 978-1-61772-121-2 (library binding)
  ISBN-10: 1-61772-121-2 (library binding)
  1. Electric fishes—Juvenile literature. 2. Platypus—Juvenile literature. I. Title.
  QL639.1.L86 2011
  591.4—dc22

                          2010034521

For more information, write to Bearport Publishing Company, Inc., 101 Fifth Avenue, Suite 6R, New York, New York 10003. Printed in the United States of America in North Mankato, Minnesota.

113010
10810CGA

10 9 8 7 6 5 4 3 2 1

Contents

The Shocking Truth

Many animals hunt and kill other animals using razor-sharp claws and teeth. Others rely on speed—pouncing, swooping, or striking out in lightning-fast attacks. Some even build traps for their victims.

Stargazer

Electric catfish

Electric eel

Certain creatures, however, have a power that no other animals have—electric power. In this book, you'll read about eight of them. Some can **electrocute** a large fish—or even a person. Others can target their victims in near-total darkness or "talk" to one another using **electricity**. Don't be too shocked by what you discover about these animals, however. After all, they do electrifying things for a good reason—to survive.

Electric ray

Platypus

Electric Eel

The electric eel is the most powerful of all electric animals. One eel can give off a 600-**volt** charge. A shock that strong is enough to kill a person!

An electric eel uses special body parts called **electric organs** to produce shocks. The skinny, snake-like fish has several pairs running along its body. Luckily, electric eels don't often attack people or large animals that enter the rivers where they live. They do, however, use their special powers to send out shocks that **stun** or kill frogs and small fish. What happens then? The **prey**— now totally powerless—are eaten by the hungry eels.

Electric eels can be up to eight feet (2.4 m) long. They live in the shallow parts of muddy rivers in South America.

An electric eel will shock a person or large animal only in order to defend itself. Most of the time, it will try to escape by swimming away instead.

Electric eels have no teeth. They hunt and eat only small animals that they can swallow whole.

Electric Ray

Rays are fish that live in the ocean and are shaped like plates. There are hundreds of different kinds, but only 69 of them are electric.

Like electric eels, electric rays use their special powers to keep enemies away and to catch prey. Unlike eels, however, rays have only one pair of electric organs—usually near their eyes. When a ray is close enough to its prey, it delivers a jolt as it wraps its flap-shaped fins around the creature. Zap—dinner is served!

electric ray

The smallest electric ray is about the size of a pancake. The largest is around six feet (1.8 m) wide. The animals hunt and eat fish as well as crabs and other shellfish.

An electric ray can produce a **discharge** of about 220 volts with its electric organs.

Unlike eels, which never chase people on purpose, rays will sometimes go after divers. Their shocks are not strong enough to kill a person, but they can be painful.

Electric Catfish

An electric catfish has large whiskers at the front of its head. These cat-like feelers may give the fish its name, but they are not the source of its electric power. That comes from a pair of large electric organs inside the middle of its body.

At up to 320 volts, the shocks that a large electric catfish can produce are very powerful. The catfish uses the shocks to zap just about any small animal that comes close as it swims in Africa's muddy rivers and lakes. As long as the unlucky creature can fit into the **predator**'s large mouth, it can become catfish food.

There are many kinds of catfish in the world, but only a few kinds can use electricity to stun other fish.

An electric catfish can be up to three feet (.9 m) long. It can catch and eat a fish up to half its own size.

barbels

A catfish's whiskers are called barbels. All catfish are able to taste as well as feel things with their barbels.

Stargazer

There are many kinds of stargazers, but only four kinds are electric. These strange-looking fish got their name because their eyes are at the top of their heads, so the fish always appear to be looking up.

All stargazers live in the ocean. They hunt by burying themselves in the sandy floor. When a fish or other sea animal passes by, the stargazer opens its large mouth and sucks the prey in.

Does a stargazer use electricity to stun its victim? Or does it send out strong electric charges only to drive off enemies? Scientists aren't completely sure. They do know, however, that this underwater sand trap can produce discharges of up to 50 volts.

Southern
stargazer

A 50-volt discharge would not be strong enough to kill the sea creatures that a stargazer hunts, but it would be enough to weaken them. The discharge would also startle but not kill an enemy.

A stargazer's electric organs are located near its eyes.

Knifefish

Electric eels, electric rays, electric catfish, and stargazers have electric organs that can send out powerful shocks. Scientists call these creatures "strongly electric" fish. Many other fish have electric organs that **generate** far less powerful shocks. Scientists call them "weakly electric."

About 30 kinds of knifefish are weakly electric. A knifefish does not produce enough electricity to stun prey. However, its low-voltage electric powers do help it catch food. How? Using its electric organs, the knifefish generates an invisible **electric field** around its body. When it swims past a shrimp or other small animal, the creature comes into the field. The knifefish can then sense the animal's size, shape, and location in the electric field—and grab a quick meal.

Electric eels and all other strongly electric fish produce electric fields around themselves. Like weakly electric fish, they use the electric fields to locate prey.

Glass knifefish

Like many other electric fish, this black ghost knifefish hunts at night. It lives in rivers and streams in South America. The fish's electric powers enable it to find food in spite of the darkness.

Elephantnose Fish

It's easy to tell how the elephantnose fish got its name. Surprisingly, though, the long "nose" on its head is not a nose at all. Instead, it is a "chin" located just below the mouth and covered with **electroreceptors**. These tiny sense organs can measure changes in the electric field made by this weakly electric fish.

An electric fish's ability to feel these changes helps it find food. However, that's not the only way the fish's electric ability helps it survive. It also helps the fish **navigate** and **communicate**. For example, an elephantnose fish sends out signals that help it find a **mate** in the muddy African rivers where it lives—even when it can't see the "nose" right in front of its face.

Every electric fish—whether its output is strong like an electric eel's or weak like the elephantnose fish's—has tiny electroreceptors spread over its body.

An electric fish's way of finding food and finding its way around with the help of electric signals is called **electrolocation**.

As it swims around at night, the elephantnose fish pokes around in the muddy river bottom for insects and worms to eat.

Great White Shark

Some fish have no electric organs and so cannot form an electric field around themselves. Yet they are still able to use electricity to zero in on a nearby animal—no matter how big or small. How is this possible?

These fish have electroreceptors that can measure other animals' electric fields, just as strongly and weakly electric fish do. The most familiar of these underwater electric meters are sharks—and the most famous shark of all is the great white. When this fierce predator catches seals, large fish, and other sea animals, it uses its huge jaws and sharp teeth as powerful weapons. However, first it has to locate its prey. For this job it gets help from a secret weapon—its built-in electric-sensing system.

Great white shark

All animals, from worms to whales to human beings, produce and use tiny amounts of electricity within their bodies. The electricity helps do jobs such as sending signals between brain cells and making muscles move. Animals with electroreceptors can sense some of the tiny electrical signals being produced by other animals that are nearby.

There are about 400 kinds of sharks. Not all of them use their electroreceptors for hunting, as the great white shark does. Some just use their electric sense to find their way as they swim.

Platypus

What has fur like a beaver's, a **bill** like a duck's, and an electric-sensing system like a shark's? The answer is a platypus.

This odd-looking **mammal** is found only in Australia. It lives at the edge of lakes and rivers. At night, the platypus dives down to the muddy bottom of the lakes and rivers, hunting for food. It closes its eyes as it swims. So how does it find the worms, insects, and shellfish that it eats? It uses electrolocation, of course!

The study of animals with electric abilities is fairly new. For example, scientists discovered the platypus's special talent only around 1980. Today, researchers are working to find out more. So be prepared. At any time, their work might produce surprising—or even shocking—discoveries.

Besides fish, only a handfu
animals can sense electrici
electroreceptors. The plat
one. Others include the **ec
which also lives in Australi
certain kinds of **salaman**

Chinese giant salamander

A platypus's
electroreceptors
are in its bill.

21

More About
Electric Animals

● Thousands of years ago in ancient Greece, doctors used electric rays to treat headaches and other medical problems. Sometimes they wrapped the fish around their patients' heads. Other times they had their patients stand on the fish in order to receive shocks from them.

○ Some aquariums have electric eels on display. Workers who handle the electric eels wear thick rubber gloves, since rubber helps protect against electric shocks.

Electric eel

● The electric eel is not a true eel. That is, it is not related to other fish that are also long and snake-like and also known as eels. This strongly electric fish is, however, closely related to the weakly electric knifefish.

○ Weakly electric fish often swim backward to grab a fish to eat. Although they can't see the prey behind them, they can sense the location of the fish using the electric field that surrounds their bodies.

Glass knifefish

● Sometimes people catching fish in the sea receive shocks when they pull in a net and touch an electric ray that has been trapped in it.

○ Rays are closely related to sharks. Like sharks, even rays that are not strongly electric have electroreceptors and can sense the electricity given off by nearby animals.

Stingray

bill (BIL) the part of a platypus's mouth that looks like the beak of some birds

communicate (kuh-MYOO-nuh-kayt) to share information

discharge (DIS-charj) a release of electrical energy

echidna (ih-KID-nuh) a small animal that lives in Australia and eats ants and termites

electric field (i-LEK-trik FEELD) an area that has electric signals

electricity (*i*-lek-TRISS-uh-tee) a form of energy that can do many different things, such as making heat and light, powering machines, and producing dangerous shocks

electric organs (i-LEK-trik OR-guhnz) the parts of an electric fish that send out powerful shocks or weaker forms of electricity

electrocute (i-LEK-truh-kyoot) to kill with electricity

electrolocation (i-*lek*-troh-loh-KAY-shuhn) the way of finding things by sensing electric signals

electroreceptors (i-*lek*-troh-rih-SEP-torz) tiny sense organs in an animal that receive electric signals

generate (JEN-ur-ayt) to produce

mammal (MAM-uhl) a warm-blooded animal that has a backbone, hair or fur on its skin, and drinks its mother's milk as a baby

mate (MAYT) one of a pair of animals that have young together

navigate (NAV-uh-gayt) to find one's way from place to place

predator (PRED-uh-tur) an animal that hunts other animals for food

prey (PRAY) animals that are hunted for food

salamanders (SAL-uh-*man*-durz) a group of animals that, like frogs, usually spend part of their lives in water and part on land

stun (STUN) to shock something so much that it is unable to move

volt (VOHLT) a unit for measuring electric strength; for example, a size-D flashlight battery can produce 1.5 volts of electricity

Index

Bibliography

Kawasaki, Masashi. "What Is an Electric Fish?" (people.virginia.edu/~mk3u/mk_lab/electric_fish_E.htm)

Nelson, Mark. "Electric Fish." (nelson.beckman.illinois.edu/electric_fish.html)

ReefQuest Centre for Shark Research. "Electric Rays: A Shocking Use of Muscle Power." (www.elasmo-research.org/education/topics/p_electric_rays.htm)

Read More

Arnold, Caroline. *Shockers of the Sea and Other Electric Animals.* Watertown, MA: Charlesbridge (1999).

Caper, William. *Platypus: A Century-long Mystery.* New York: Bearport (2009).

Landau, Elaine. *Electric Fish.* New York: Children's Press (1999).

Van Dyck, Sara. *Electric Eels.* Minneapolis, MN: Lerner (2008).

Learn More Online

To learn more about electric animals, visit
www.bearportpublishing.com/AnimalswithSuperPowers

About the Author

Natalie Lunis lives in the Hudson River Valley, just north of New York City. She has written two books about electricity and many books about animals. This is her first book about electric animals.